science fair

j 537.087
L 379e

OCT -- 2002

Science Alive!
Electricity

CRABTREE
Publishing Company
www.crabtreebooks.com

How to use this book

Each chapter begins with experiments, followed by the explanation of the scientific concepts used in the experiments. Each experiment is graded according to its difficulty level. A level 4 or 5 means adult assistance is advised. Difficult words are in boldface and explained in the glossary on page 32.

Crabtree Publishing
www.crabtreebooks.com

PMB 16A, 350 Fifth Avenue,
Suite 3308, New York
New York 10118

612 Welland Avenue,
St. Catharines, Ontario,
Canada L2M 5V6

**Published in 2002
by Crabtree Publishing Company**

Published with Times Editions
Copyright © 2002 by Times Media Private Limited

Series originated and designed by
TIMES EDITIONS
An imprint of Times Media Private Limited
A member of the Times Publishing Group

Coordinating Editor: Ellen Rodger
Project Editors: P. A. Finlay, Carrie Gleason
Production Coordinator: Rosie Gowsell
Series Writers: Darlene Lauw, Lim Cheng Puay
Series Editors: Oh Hwee Yen, Scott Marsh
Series Designers: Loo Chuan Ming, Lynn Chin
Series Picture Researcher: Susan Jane Manuel
Series Illustrator: Roy Chan Yoon Loy

Cataloging-in-Publication Data
Lauw, Darlene.
 Electricity / Darlene Lauw & Lim Cheng Puay.
  p. cm. — (Science alive)
 Includes index.
 Summary: Presents activities that demonstrate how electricity works
in our everyday lives. History boxes feature the scientists who made
significant discoveries in the field of electricity.
 ISBN 0-7787-0561-7 (RLB) — ISBN 0-7787-0607-9 (pbk.)
 1. Electricity—Experiments—Juvenile literature. [1. Electricity—Experiments.
2. Experiments.] I. Puay, Lim Cheng. II. Title.
 QC527.2 .L38 2002
 537'.078—dc21

2001042421
LC

Picture Credits

Marc Crabtree: cover; Bes Stock: 6, 14, 22; Getty Images/ Hulton Archives: 23 (bottom); Hutchison Library: 15 (bottom); Science Photo Library: 10, 11 (both), 15 (top), 18, 19, 23 (top), 26, 27 (both), 30, 31; Tettoni Photography: 1, 7

Printed and bound in Malaysia
1 2 3 4 5 6—0S—07 06 05 04 03 02

INTRODUCTION

How does an electrical circuit work? How can lemons power a light bulb? What are electrical conductors and insulators? These questions relate to electricity. Electricity is a natural form of energy that humans use to power their lights, computers, cars, and more. Learn more about electricity by doing the science experiments in this book.

Contents

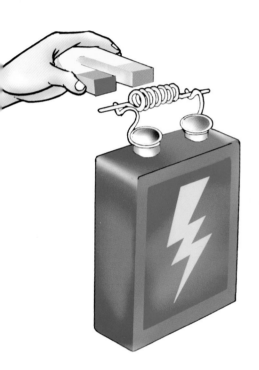

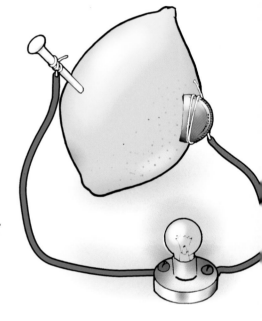

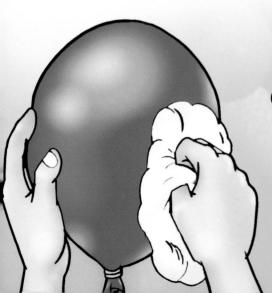

Make your own electrical circuit!

Electricity can only flow in a loop called a **circuit**. When a circuit is closed, electricity flows through wires to power an electrical device such as a light bulb. This experiment will show you how to make a simple electrical circuit.

Difficult — 5
— 4
Moderate — 3
— 2
Easy — 1

You will need:
- Tape
- A piece of pencil lead
- A flat tabletop
- A nine-volt battery
- A light bulb and holder
- Three pieces of insulated wire, each 12 inches (30 cm) long

Wire circuit

1 Tape the piece of pencil lead to the tabletop.

2 Join one battery terminal to the bulb with wire 1. Join the other terminal to the pencil lead with wire 2. Join the pencil lead to the bulb with wire 3. The bulb lights up because the circuit is closed.

wire 1

wire 2 — wire 3

3 Slowly slide wire 3 along the pencil lead in a left–right motion. The light glows more brightly!

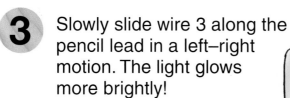

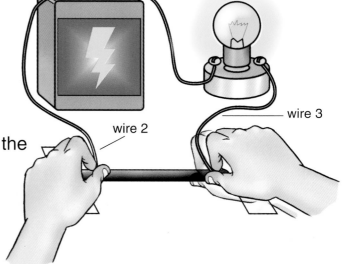

wire 1

wire 2 — wire 3

Steady hand game

■ Ask an adult
for help

Difficult — 5
       4
Moderate — 3
       2
Easy — 1

You will need:
- A wire coat hanger
- A pair of pliers
- A shoe box
- Plasticine
- Tape
- A light bulb and holder
- Three pieces of insulated wire 12 inches (30 cm) long
- A nine-volt battery
- A wooden stick 6 inches (15 cm) long

1 Ask an adult to snap the hook off the coat hanger using the pliers. Twist the coat hanger into the shape shown below. Insert both ends of the twisted coat hanger into the shoe box. Use the plasticine to secure the ends of the hanger to the box. Tape the light bulb holder and battery to the top of the shoe box as shown.

2 Wrap one end of wire 1 around the base of the left side of the coat hanger. Attach the other end of wire 1 to a battery terminal. Use wire 2 to join the other battery terminal to the light bulb holder.

3 Attach one end of wire 3 to the other side of the light bulb holder.

4 Bend the coat hanger hook into a tight loop around the wire frame. Push the end of the loop into the wooden stick.

5 Attach the free end of wire 3 to the coat hanger loop.

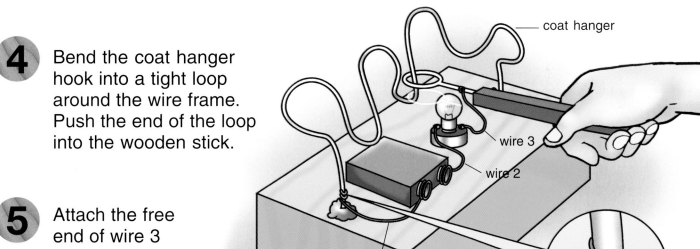

coat hanger
wire 3
wire 2
wire 1

6 If the loop touches the coat hanger, this will close the circuit and the light bulb will light up. Now, test how steady your hand is! Try to move the loop from one end of the bent wire to the other end without lighting the bulb.

How does electricity move?

The *Wire Circuit* and *Steady Hand Game* experiments showed how electricity had to flow in a continuous loop to power the light bulb. This continuous flow of electricity is called a closed circuit. In the *Steady Hand Game* experiment, the coat hanger loop had to touch the frame to close the circuit. This is because electricity flows through a circuit in currents. Currents are made up of tiny **particles** called **electrons**. When a source of power, such as a battery, is connected to a circuit, electrons bump against one another through the circuit to the light bulb. If there is a gap in the circuit, it is called an open circuit. When the circuit is open, the bumping of electrons stops, so the current does not reach the light bulb. Switches can control an electrical current, just like the coat hanger loop controlled the current in the *Steady Hand Game* experiment.

Electrical currents are measured in **amperes** (A). The ability of a power source, such as a battery, to produce an electrical current is measured in volts (V). Electrical currents flow like water down a hill. The flow is known as potential. The potential of electrical currents is its strength, or the "push" of the flowing charge or volt.

Electricity powers many items in your home such as alarm clocks and light bulbs.

Who discovered how electricity travels?

Benjamin Franklin (1706–1790) was an American writer, scientist, diplomat, and statesman. As a scientist, Franklin experimented with electricity.

Franklin thought that lightning was an electrical current found in nature. To test his theory, Franklin decided to see if lightning would pass through an electrical conductor such as metal. In 1752, he attached a kite to a metal spike in the ground and let the kite fly high during a thunderstorm. He had tied a metal key to the tail of the kite. Whenever lightning struck the kite's metal key, a spark would jump from the spike! This experiment showed that lightning was a form of electricity. It also showed that electricity could flow from one point to another.

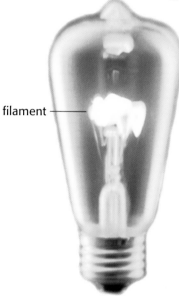

filament

Did you know?
Certain types of fish, such as electric eels, produce electricity! An electric eel has thousands of special muscles in its body. Each of these muscles produces a small electrical charge. Together, the muscles can produce a large electrical charge. Electric eels can produce an electrical charge of 300 to 650 volts! These electrical charges help electric eels stun their prey while hunting. They are also used in self-defense, and to help eels move from place to place.

HANDLE WITH CARE!

You should always be careful when using electrical appliances. Even a small current leak in a circuit can give you an electric shock! You should never touch exposed wires. Never turn on electrical switches if your fingers are wet. The water on your fingers could cause the electrical charges to flow through you instead of through the wires!

Electrical conductors and insulators

Have you ever wondered why electrical wires are covered with a layer of plastic? Why are electrical wires made of metal? Here is a simple experiment to find out the answer!

Difficult — 5
— 4
Moderate — 3
— 2
Easy — 1

You will need:
- A six-volt battery
- Two copper wires, each 6 inches (15 cm) long
- A light bulb and holder
- A paper clip
- A wooden pencil
- An eraser
- A plastic spoon

Electric stoppers

1 Set up the circuit as shown. Leave a gap between the two exposed ends of the wires so that the circuit is open.

2 Place the paper clip in the gap. Now, touch the exposed ends of the wires to the paper clip. Does the bulb light up?

3 Do the same with the other materials. Which materials cause the bulb to light up?

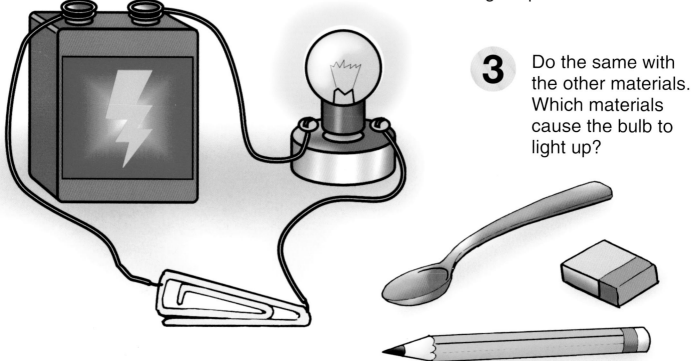

Now you know that electrical currents can only pass through some materials. These materials are known as electrical conductors. Which materials conduct electricity best?

Difficult — 5
— 4
Moderate — 3
— 2
Easy — 1

You will need:
- Electrical circuit from previous experiment
- Aluminum foil
- A steel nail
- An iron nail
- A nickel

Resistance

1 Set up the circuit again.

2 Place the aluminum foil in the gap. Observe the brightness of the bulb.

3 Do the same with the other materials. Which material makes the bulb glow the brightest?

Conductors and insulators

An electrical current is made up of electrons moving in a circuit. Electrons are tiny bits of negative electricity that are found in all **matter**. In certain materials such as iron, electrons can move freely. These materials are good electrical conductors.

In materials such as plastic, electrons are attached to larger particles and cannot move freely. These materials do not conduct electricity well, and are called non-conductors, or insulators. This was why the plastic spoon did not allow the electrical current to pass through in the *Electric Stoppers* experiment.

There are two kinds of electricity: positive and negative. Electrical charges only attract opposites. Negative charges attract positive charges. Two positive charges will resist each other. Resistance measures how much a substance opposes the flow of electricity. In the *Resistance* experiment, some conductors worked better than others. The materials that did not conduct well, such as the pencil lead, had a high resistance to electricity.

Power lines are made from materials with low electrical resistance, such as aluminum, because they are used to carry enormous amounts of electricity.

Ohm's Law

Georg Simon Ohm (1787–1854) was a German **physicist** who discovered the relationship between current, voltage, and resistance. Ohm found that the flow of electrical currents was faster when their voltages were increased. Electrical currents slow down when flowing through conductors with a high resistance. Ohm's research uncovered the law of basic current flow, which is now used for electrical circuit design. This law is now known as Ohm's Law. The basic unit for measuring resistance is also named the **ohm**.

QUIZTIME

Starting with the poorest conductor, rank the metals listed below according to how well they conduct electricity.
Gold, copper, graphite, wood, mercury, glass

Answer: Glass, wood, graphite, mercury, copper, gold

Did you know?

All materials conduct electricity to a certain degree. A good conductor of electricity, such as copper or silver, can conduct electricity a billion times better than a bad conductor such as glass! When certain substances, such as tin and aluminum, are cooled to -32°F (0°C) and below, they no longer have any electrical resistance. These substances are known as superconductors.

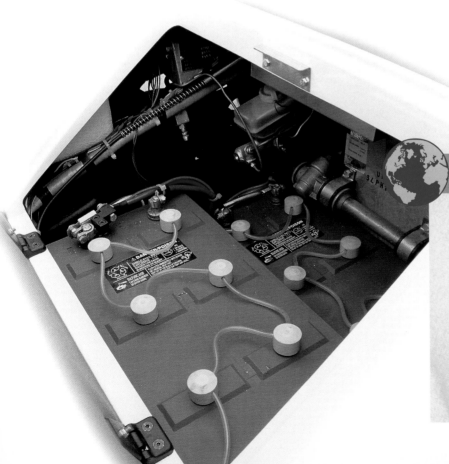

ELECTRIC CARS

Electric cars use electric motors powered by large batteries (*left*). The electric motor in the car converts electrical energy into kinetic energy, or the energy of motion. To drive backward, you use a switch to change the direction of the flow of electricity. This makes the electric motor turn in the opposite direction, and makes the car move backward.

Static electricity

T he electricity that powers the machines in your home is made by generators in power stations. You can generate small amounts of electricity without any special equipment! Try these experiments to generate electricity.

Difficult — 5
— 4
Moderate — 3
— 2
Easy — 1

You will need:
- A balloon
- A piece of woolen cloth
- Small pieces of paper
- A piece of cotton cloth
- A comb or brush
- A plastic pen

Static electricity

1 Blow up the balloon. Rub it against the piece of woolen cloth. Hold the balloon against a wall and let go of it. Does the balloon cling to the wall?

2 The balloon, now charged with static electricity, can also pick up pieces of paper! Try rubbing the balloon against the piece of cotton cloth to see which material gives the greatest charge. The greater the charge, the more pieces of paper the balloon can pick up.

3 You can also generate static electricity by combing your hair. Try rubbing the plastic pen with a piece of cloth. Now see if you can make your hair stand up with the pen.

Bending water

You will need:
- A tap
- Two plastic pens
- A piece of cloth
- Two small bottle corks
- A tub of water
- A friend

1 Run a slow stream of cold water from the tap. Make the stream as slow as it will go before it begins to drip.

2 Now, rub the dry plastic pen with the piece of cloth. Bring the pen as close as you can to the stream of water without touching it. The stream will "bend" as the charged pen attracts the water.

Boat race game

1 Each player needs a small bottle cork as a boat. Float your boats in a large tub of water.

NOTE
Remember to keep the pens dry, or they will lose their electrical charge.

2 Rub your dry plastic pens with the cloth. Bring the pens as close as you can to the boats without touching them. What do you see? The static charge from your pens moves the boats!

What is static electricity?

Static electricity is an electrical charge that is stationary, meaning that it does not move. Static charges remain on an insulator, such as the balloon in the *Static Electricity* experiment. The electrical charge does not flow as it would in a closed circuit.

There are two kinds of electrical charges: positive and negative. Each charge attracts its opposite. Positive attracts negative and repels other positives. Electrons are negatively charged particles. Positively charged particles are called protons. When a balloon is rubbed against a piece of cloth, the negative electrons from the cloth move to the balloon. The balloon is now negatively charged. Since the cloth lost some of its electrons, it is now positively charged. The negatively charged balloon will now stick to another object, such as a wall, that has all its protons and electrons in place.

In the *Bending Water* experiment, the pen gained a negative charge from the electrons it took from the cloth. When you put the pen beside the water, the water bent. This happened because the water still had all of its electrons and protons. In other words, the water was **neutral**.

Non-conducting materials such as balloons can store static electricity.

Who discovered static electricity?

Around 600 B.C. a Greek philosopher named Thales (*left*) discovered static electricity. He found that if he rubbed a hard **fossilized** material known as amber against a cloth, the amber would pick up pieces of straw. This strange effect remained a mystery for about 2,000 years.

In 1600 A.D. Dr. William Gilbert investigated different materials and came up with a list of materials that could be electrically charged when rubbed. He also realized that static electricity only occurs in dry air. The presence of moisture would conduct electricity away to the Earth and prevent electrical charges from accumulating on the surface of an object.

QUIZTIME

Why are non-conducting materials needed to generate static electricity?

Answer: Non-conductors allow charges to accumulate on their surface. If a conducting material is used, electrons will not collect on the surface but will be conducted through the object.

Did you know?
Electric generators are machines that produce electricity. A generator is powered by an engine that produces mechanical energy. This mechanical energy is then converted into electrical energy. Some generators used in scientific instruments are so small they can fit into the palm of your hand. Other generators are bigger than your house! These generators provide electricity to run machines in offices and factories as well as the electrical devices found in your home.

GROUNDING CABLES

When a gasoline truck fills the underground tanks at a gas station, the transfer of gasoline from the truck to the tank can produce electrical charges. This is very dangerous as one spark of static electricity could ignite the gasoline. Grounding cables are used to conduct electrical charges to the Earth, to prevent any sparks from forming.

Electricity detectors

W ith a magnet and a few coils of wire, you can make your own electricity detector.

You will need:
- Tape
- Two magnets
- Two bookends
- A rectangular block of wood
- A knitting needle
- Two thick pieces of cardboard
- A small box
- A straw
- Scissors
- PVC insulated wire, 13 feet (4 m) long
- Thumbtacks
- A six-volt battery

Making a galvanometer

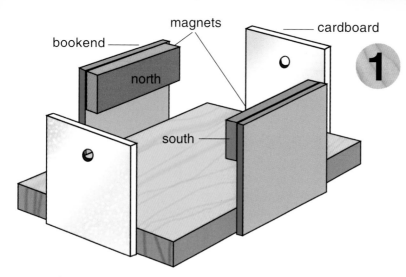

magnets
bookend
cardboard
north
south

1 Tape each magnet onto a bookend. Place the bookends on opposite sides of the wood block. The attracting ends of the two magnets should face each other.

2 Use the knitting needle to punch a hole in each piece of cardboard. The knitting needle must fit into the opening with room to spare. Tape the cardboard pieces to the wood block as shown.

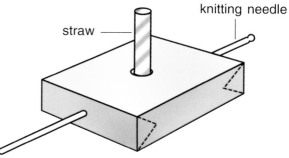

straw
knitting needle

3 Make a hole at the center of the box and insert the straw into it. Cut a V-shaped piece from each corner of the box. Push the knitting needle through the sides of the box.

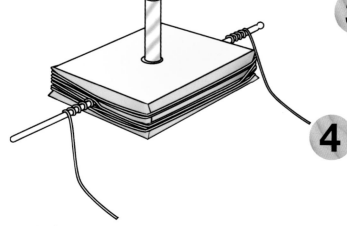

4 Wrap the wire around the box, then coil the ends of the wire around the knitting needle. Leave about 20 inches (50 cm) of loose wire at each end.

5 Insert the knitting needle into the holes of the cardboard ends. Pin the ends of the wire onto the board with the tacks. Level the box with the wood block.

6 Tape the ends of the wire to the battery to form a circuit. Does the box move now that a current is passing through it?

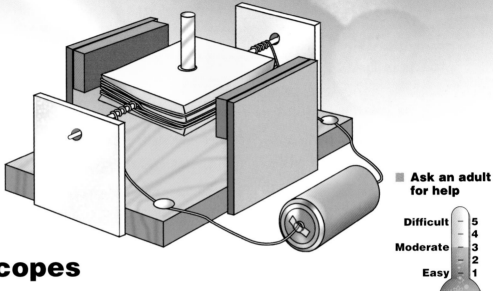

■ **Ask an adult for help**

Difficult — 5
— 4
Moderate — 3
— 2
Easy — 1

Electroscopes

Electroscopes are used to test for small electrical charges, especially static charges. You can make your own electroscope using materials found at home!

You will need:
- A copper wire 8 inches (20 cm) long
- A glass jar
- A strip of aluminum foil 4 inches (10 cm) long
- An aluminum pie plate
- A comb

1 Ask an adult to help you bend the copper wire into the shape of a "Z." Hang it over the edge of the jar. Fold the foil strip in half and hang it over the part of the copper wire that is in the jar.

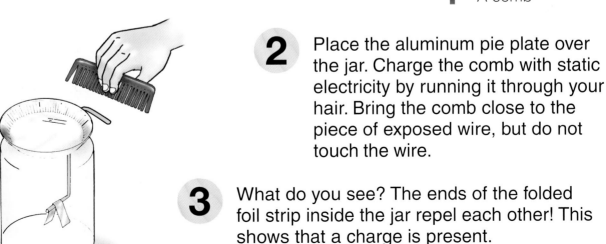

2 Place the aluminum pie plate over the jar. Charge the comb with static electricity by running it through your hair. Bring the comb close to the piece of exposed wire, but do not touch the wire.

3 What do you see? The ends of the folded foil strip inside the jar repel each other! This shows that a charge is present.

Magnets, electricity, and galvanometers

A magnet is an object that can push or pick up things made of iron, steel, or nickel. Magnets are found in nature, but can also be made. A current of electricity can also produce magnetism. Magnets have a north and a south pole. When the north pole of one magnet is facing the south pole of a second magnet, the force between the two magnets pulls them together. This force is called a magnetic field. In the *Making a Galvanometer* experiment, the copper coil created a magnetic field when it was hooked up to the battery. The copper coil had a north and south pole, just like the magnets. The attraction of the south end of the coil to the north pole of the magnet caused the copper coil and the box to move.

Galvanometers are instruments that **detect** and measure small electrical currents. The strength of the current is shown by the movement of a magnetic needle or coil in a magnetic field. The stronger the magnetic force, the more the needle moves.

These devices are galvanometers, which are used to detect and measure electrical currents.

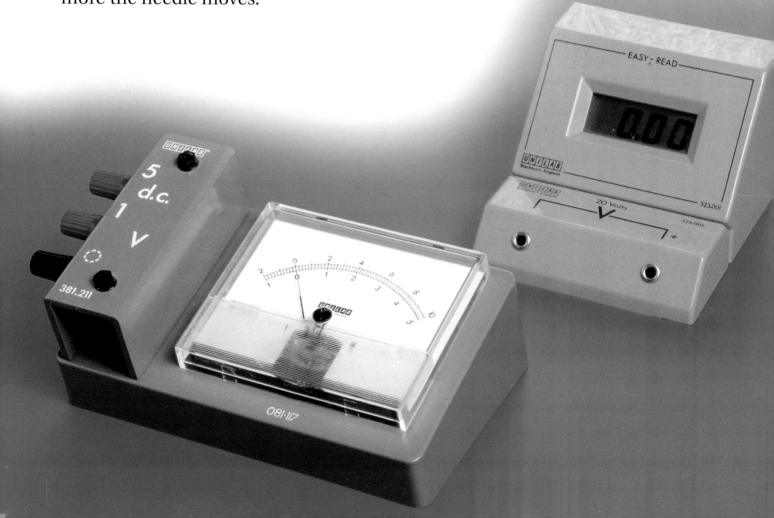

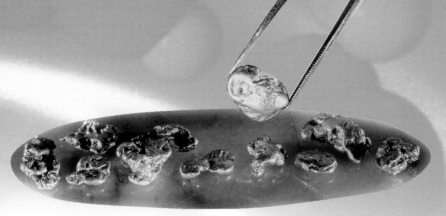

Gold is used in scientific electroscopes.

Electroscopes and static electricity

An electroscope is used to detect static electricity. It can also show how strong an electrical charge is. In the *Electroscopes* experiment, the separation, or repulsion, of the ends of the aluminum strip showed that a charge was present. How did that happen? When you ran the comb through your hair, you charged it with negative charges. When you brought the comb near the wire, the negative charges in the wire moved away from the comb toward the aluminum strip. Both ends of the aluminum strip were then filled with negative charges. The negative charges repelled each other and the ends of the strip moved apart.

Some scientific electroscopes use thin pieces of gold instead of aluminum to detect electrical charges. These devices are called gold-leaf electroscopes.

QUIZTIME

If a neutral object is placed near either a positively or negatively charged gold-leaf electroscope, what will happen to the leaf?

Answer: A neutral object has equal amounts of positive and negative charges. In a negatively charged electroscope, the electrons will move toward the positive charges in the object. This results in less repulsion between the leaf and the plate. A positively charged electroscope will attract electrons from the neutral object. This reduces the positive charge, resulting in less repulsion as well.

Did you know?

Lightning is produced when static electricity in clouds is discharged. In a storm, the charges in a cloud are separated. Negative charges gather at the bottom of the cloud and positive charges gather at the top. The ground below the cloud has more positive charges than the bottom of the cloud. There is an attraction between the ground and the bottom of the cloud. This means that electrons near the cloud will be pulled down toward the ground. This is how lightning is created!

STATIC AT WORK

Photocopying machines use static electricity. The machine scans the dark parts of a page which is then electrically charged on a roller. When a sheet of paper passes the roller, static electricity drags carbon powder onto the paper. The powder is heated and attached onto the paper. This is why the paper feels hot when it first comes out of the machine!

19

Create your own power source!

A battery is an amazing invention. It allows us to carry a portable energy source around. Try making your own battery in this experiment.

■ Ask an adult for help

Difficult – 5
– 4
Moderate – 3
– 2
Easy – 1

You will need:
- A lemon
- A pocketknife
- A clean, galvanized nail
- A coin
- Two copper wires
- A small light bulb and holder

Lemon battery

 Citric acid is found in lemons. In this experiment, it has to move around freely within the fruit. Break down the lemon's cell structure by squeezing it hard or dropping it on the floor. Be careful not to split the skin!

2 Ask an adult to make two slits in the lemon skin using the pocketknife. Put the nail in one slit and the coin in the other. Do not let the two metal objects touch inside the lemon.

3 Wrap one end of a copper wire around the nail. Then wrap one end of the other copper wire around the coin.

4 Connect the loose ends of the copper wires to the light bulb holder. What do you see? The bulb lights up!

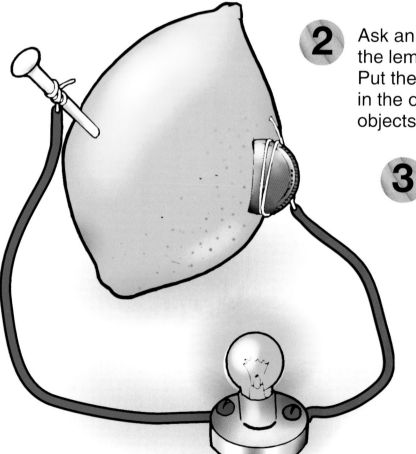

Sometimes, the lemon battery may not provide enough power. Do not give up! You can try vinegar instead.

Difficult — 5
— 4
Moderate — 3
— 2
Easy — 1

You will need:
- Two copper wires
- Three clean, galvanized nails
- A coin
- A small light bulb and holder
- A glass of vinegar
- Tape

Vinegar battery

1 Wrap one end of a copper wire around the three galvanized nails. Wrap the other copper wire around the coin.

2 Connect the two wires to the small light bulb holder.

3 Now put the nails and the coin in the glass of vinegar. Tape the wires to the sides of the glass. It is important that the wires are in contact with all the nails and the coin, and that the wires are not dipped into the vinegar. The bulb should now light up!

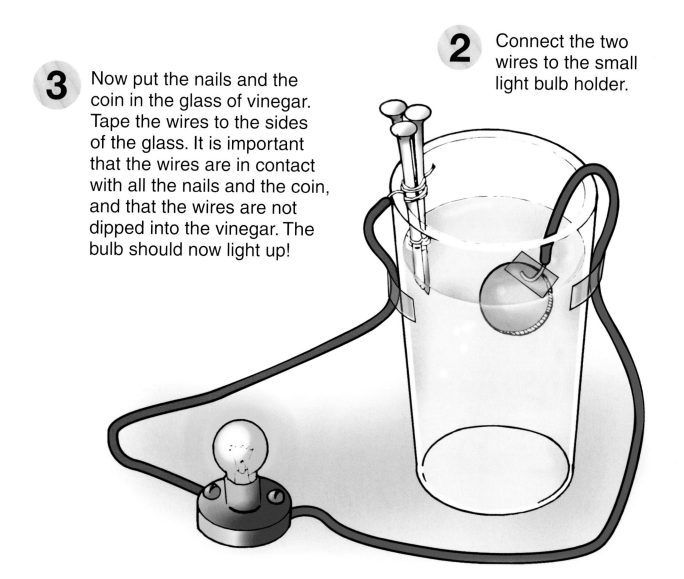

How does a battery work?

A battery works by converting chemical energy into electrical energy. Chemical energy is found in the bonds that hold molecules together in foods and other chemical substances. For example, when we eat, we are breaking down these bonds in our food, which gives us energy.

The *Lemon Battery* and *Vinegar Battery* experiments used two types of metals, the coin and the nails, and citric acid to release chemical energy. The batteries used the metals, called the **electrodes**, to cause a chemical reaction in the citric acid, called the **electrolyte**. When hooked up to the circuit, the electrodes broke down the chemical bonds in the electrolyte which caused electrons to be released. The two electrodes, the nails and the coin, became electrically charged by the electrons. The electrons in the negatively charged electrode traveled down the wire to the positively charged electrode. This current of electrons is what lit the bulb!

Without batteries, even gasoline-powered vehicles like this off-road buggy would not be able to start!

⊙QUIZTIME

If similar poles of two batteries are positioned facing each other, will the batteries work?

Answer: No current will be produced by the batteries because the current has to travel from a negative to a positive pole.

Household batteries work in the same way!

The batteries that we use in our flashlights, toys, and other battery-operated machines use the same principle as the lemon and vinegar batteries in the experiments. The electrodes usually consist of a zinc casing and a carbon rod. The electrolyte used is not a liquid but a sticky paste. This is why such batteries are called dry-cell batteries. This type of battery has a larger current than the "wet" battery you made.

A battery-operated toy

Did you know?

Battery technology is so advanced that batteries are powerful enough to power cars. Instead of gasoline, batteries supply power to electric engines. These electric cars may be more common in the future as alternatives to gasoline-powered vehicles.

PROTECTING APPLIANCES

You should never leave batteries in battery-operated objects when they are not in use. If unused batteries are left in battery-operated appliances for too long, their cells will start to break down. This may cause the chemicals in the batteries to leak and damage the electrical devices.

Electric motors

Magnets can attract electrical wires and electricity can make magnets move. Find out how by doing these experiments.

■ **Ask an adult for help**

Difficult — 5
— 4
Moderate — 3
— 2
Easy — 1

You will need:
- A copper wire 10–12 inches (25–30 cm) long
- A pencil
- A pair of pliers
- Two paper clips
- A six-volt battery
- Sandpaper
- A magnet

Simple electric motor

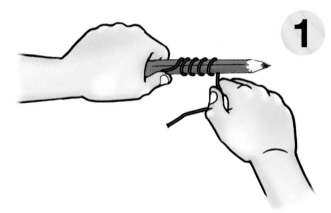

1 Wrap the copper wire around the pencil to form a coil. Remove the pencil from the coil. Leave 4 inches (10 cm) of straight wire at each end.

2 With the pliers, bend the paper clips into an "S" shape. Then wrap the bottom end of each paper clip around a battery terminal as shown below.

3 Rub both ends of the wire with sandpaper to increase their conductivity. Place the coiled wire on the paper clips as shown on the right.

4 Now hold the magnet near the wire. Do you see the copper wire rotating? Why?

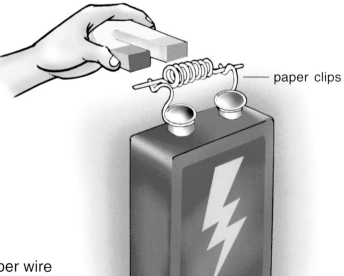

paper clips

 CAUTION
Do not touch the copper wire after you have placed it on the paper clips. You may get a small electric shock!

24

Magnets can move wires that have electrical currents flowing through them. How does electricity move magnets?

☐ **Ask an adult for help**

Difficult — 5
— 4
Moderate — 3
— 2
Easy — 1

You will need:
- Plastic-covered copper wire
- Wire cutters
- A nine-volt battery
- A piece of string
- A small magnet
- Tape
- A wooden ruler
- Four heavy books
- A small light bulb and a holder

Moving magnet

1 Ask an adult to cut two pieces of copper wire 4 inches (10 cm) long, and use the wire cutter to remove about 1/2 inch (1.3 cm) of the plastic from both ends of the wire.

2 Set up the circuit as shown below. Do not connect any wires to the battery's negative terminal.

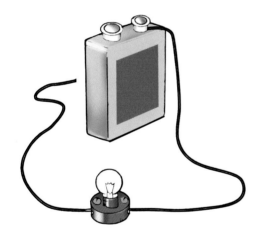

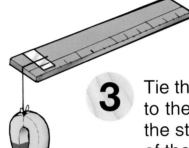

3 Tie the piece of string to the magnet. Tape the string to the end of the ruler.

4 Place the untaped end of the ruler between the books. The magnet should hang about 1 inch (2.5 cm) above the circuit.

5 Place the wire connecting the battery to the light bulb holder in a straight line below the magnet.

6 Now touch the free wire to the battery's negative terminal. Does the magnet swing when the bulb is lit?

Magnetism from electricity!

When you connected or closed the circuit in the *Simple Electric Motor* and *Moving Magnet* experiments, the electrical current flowed through the wires. This current produced a magnetic field. The magnet would only have moved if the magnetic field was strong enough. The wire carrying the electrical current behaved like a magnet. It either attracted or repelled the magnet hanging above it. If the direction of the current was changed by switching the wires, the direction of the magnetic field would also have changed. Try this to see if there are any changes in the way the magnet moves.

When you conduct the *Moving Magnet* experiment, it is important to lay the wire flat below the magnet. Magnetic fields form in **concentric** circles around a current-carrying wire. Laying the wire flat ensures that the strongest part of the wire's magnetic field interacts with the magnet.

Large waterfalls produce energy. This energy is used to create hydroelectricity.

Electromagnetic energy

Danish physicist Hans Christian Oersted (*left*) first observed the magnetic field produced by an electrical current in 1819. In 1821, the English physicist and chemist, Michael Faraday (1791–1867) plotted the magnetic field around an electrical current. Faraday also discovered **electromagnetic induction** in 1831. Electromagnetic induction is the creation of an electrical current when a conductor comes in contact with a magnetic field.

Peter's brother played a trick on him. He placed a plastic strip that looks identical to Peter's electrical wire in a box containing Peter's moving magnet experiment. How can Peter find the real wire using just the battery and the light bulb?

Answer: Set up the circuit with each wire and see which one lights up the bulb. Since plastic does not conduct electricity well, the bulb will not light up when it is connected to the plastic strip.

Did you know?

About a quarter of the energy produced worldwide comes from hydroelectricity. Hydroelectricity is a renewable source of energy, unlike the energy from fossil fuels. Other sources of energy humans use to generate electricity include steam plants, nuclear energy, and burning fuels.

SOLAR ENERGY

Solar energy comes from the sun. It is a clean and almost unlimited source of energy. People use devices known as solar cells to collect energy from the sun's rays. Solar cells change the sun's energy into electrical energy. Other devices known as flat-plate collectors change solar energy into heat energy. This energy can be used to heat the air and water inside buildings.

Making electricity

C hemicals like citric acid can produce electricity. You can also produce electricity using magnets. Here's how!

You will need:
- A copper wire 8 inches (20 cm) long
- A magnet
- A galvanometer
- Tape
- A piece of string 8 inches (20 cm) long

Electrifying magnets

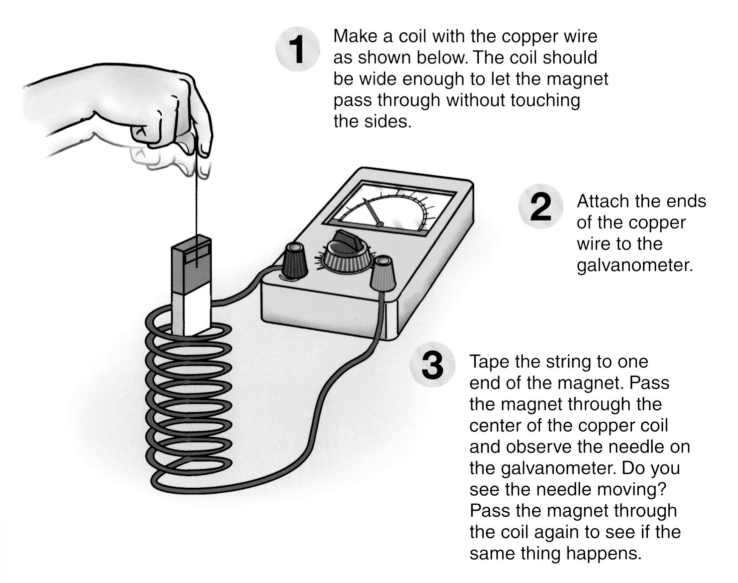

1 Make a coil with the copper wire as shown below. The coil should be wide enough to let the magnet pass through without touching the sides.

2 Attach the ends of the copper wire to the galvanometer.

3 Tape the string to one end of the magnet. Pass the magnet through the center of the copper coil and observe the needle on the galvanometer. Do you see the needle moving? Pass the magnet through the coil again to see if the same thing happens.

Heat can also generate electricity. Scientists have used this knowledge to make thermometers.

Difficult — 5
— 4
Moderate — 3
— 2
Easy — 1

Hot electricity

1 Set up the circuit as shown below. Use the pliers to twist the ends of the iron and copper wires together.

2 Dip one end of the circuit into the glass of ice water.

3 Dip the other end of the circuit into the glass of hot water.

4 Observe the needle in the galvanometer. Do you see the needle move?

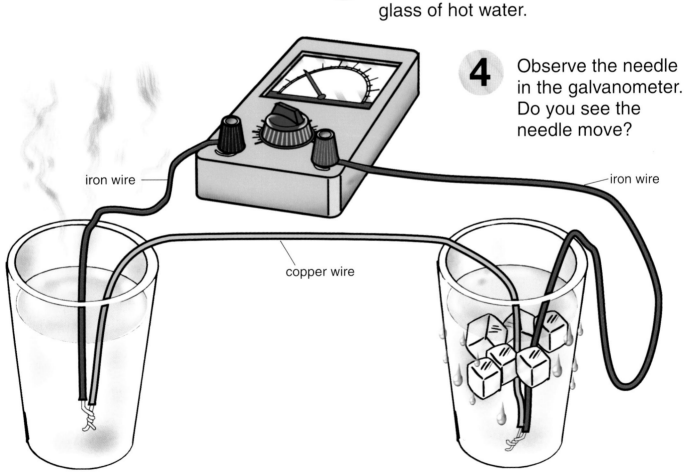

iron wire

iron wire

copper wire

Electrifying magnets

The copper wire used in the *Electrifying Magnets* experiment contained free electrons. Free electrons are not attached to any type of particle. Free electrons can move when placed near external electric or magnetic fields. When the magnet was placed inside the copper coil, the magnetic field of the magnet caused the free electrons to move through the copper wire. Their movement produced electricity. This is known as electromagnetic induction.

In the *Hot Electricity* experiment, you made a **thermocouple**. It used two wires of different metals twisted together to create an electrical effect. One end of the twisted wires, known as a junction, was heated by placing it in hot water. The other junction was cooled by placing it in cold water. The temperature difference between the two junctions created an electrical current.

Flashes of lightning are like huge sparks of electricity!

The Seebeck Effect

In 1821, German physicist Thomas Seebeck discovered that an electrical current is produced when the ends of two different metals are kept at different temperatures. Seebeck joined a strip of copper to a strip of bismuth, a type of metal, to form a closed circuit. The circuit had two junctions, each where the two metal strips joined. Seebeck found that an electrical current was created when he heated one junction. The current flowed around the circuit as long as there was a temperature difference.

Seebeck found that this happened with any pair of metals. He also found that the amount of current produced is related to the temperature difference at each junction. The greater the temperature difference, the higher the voltage. Scientists credit his discovery by naming it the Seebeck Effect.

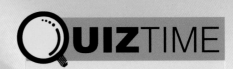

How do thermocouples measure temperature?

Answer: A thermocouple used to measure temperature has two junctions. One junction is kept at a constant temperature. The other junction is heated to the temperature being measured. When the two junctions are at different temperatures, an electrical current is produced. A voltmeter measures the current produced between the junctions and changes this information into a temperature reading.

Did you know?

Thermocouples are instruments used to measure temperature. They are more accurate than glass thermometers because metals conduct heat better than glass. A thermocouple produces a small voltage when there is a temperature difference between two metals. Different metals are combined to measure different temperature ranges. For example, a thermocouple made of copper and iron can be used to measure temperatures up to 500°F (260°C).

ELECTRICITY FROM HEAT

Thermoelectric generators produce electricity based on the concept of the thermocouple. On one side of the generator, a gas burner maintains the temperature at about 1004°F (540°C). Aluminum coolers on the opposite side of the generator keep the temperature at about 284°F (140°C). These generators can produce electrical currents of up to 5,000 watts!

Glossary

ampere (page 6): The standard unit for measuring an electrical current.

circuit (page 4): The complete path of an electrical current. This usually includes the source of electrical energy, such as a battery.

citric acid (page 20): A weak acid found in fruits such as lemons.

concentric (page 26): Sharing a common center.

detect (page 18): To discover the presence or existence of something.

electrode (page 22): The part of a battery where an electrical current enters or leaves the battery.

electrolyte (page 22): A substance that can conduct electricity.

electromagnetic induction (page 27): The creation of an electrical current when a conductor moves across a magnetic field.

electrons (page 6): Tiny bits of negative electricity that are found in all matter.

electroscopes (page 17): Devices that check for the presence of electrical charges.

fossilized (page 15): Describes the remains of ancient animals or plants that have turned into minerals.

matter (page 10): Any substance that occupies space and has mass.

neutral (page 14): Uncharged objects.

ohm (page 11): The basic unit for measuring electrical resistance.

particle (page 6): One of the basic units of matter, such as an electron.

physicist (page 11): A scientist who specializes in the study of physics.

thermocouple (page 30): A device that uses wires of two different metals to take temperature readings.

Index